To my dear Ida, in times, good times and sad times. My prayers and love go out to you.

Lanell

I'll always be your friend

As I Look Out of My Kitchen Window

I know this lady personally. She's a beautiful lady!

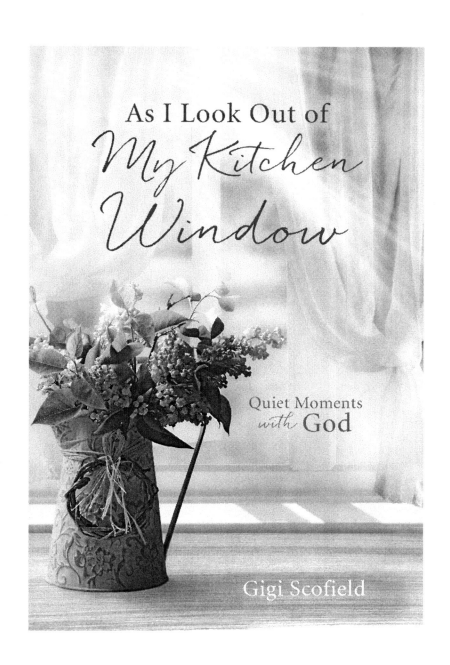

Xulon Press
2301 Lucien Way #415
Maitland, FL 32751
407.339.4217
www.xulonpress.com

© 2017 by Gigi Scofield

All rights reserved solely by the author. The author guarantees all contents are original and do not infringe upon the legal rights of any other person or work. No part of this book may be reproduced in any form without the permission of the author. The views expressed in this book are not necessarily those of the publisher.

Unless otherwise indicated, Scripture quotations taken from the New American Standard Bible (NASB). Copyright © 1960, 1962, 1963, 1968, 1971, 1972, 1973, 1975, 1977, 1995 by The Lockman Foundation. Used by permission. All rights reserved.

Printed in the United States of America.

ISBN: 9781545616604

WHAT GOD HAS REVEALED TO ME, AS I LOOK OUT OF MY KITCHEN WINDOW.

Regular time spent at my sink and looking out of my kitchen window has given me many opportunities to see, and to understand, God's amazing beauty; His great love and faithfulness, His gracious gifts, and His marvelous creation. Over the years I have had many conversations with my Lord, as I looked out of this small, wood framed window. It has been a quiet place where I have routinely slowed down long enough to talk to, but also listen to, my Heavenly Father. I am thankful for the ways He has revealed Himself to me in the routine, familiar, and quiet moments—

As I prayed while looking out of my kitchen window.

Acknowledgements

I would like to express my great appreciation to those who have given me the courage, support and a reason to write.

Darcie, you have patiently walked with me through the process of writing this book from the moment it began. Your prayers, counsel and constant belief in what God was doing has been a source of godly influence and love. Thank you my dear friend and sister in Christ.

Carrie and Tracie, I am grateful for the encouragement I received from both of you. Your timely words of advice and support have meant more than either of you could ever know.

To my children and grandchildren (Jon and Doni; Nate, McKenzi, Madison, Peyton, Noah and Gracie; Aaron, Alicia, Titus and Eli): you inspire me as I watch and love you. Each of you are a gift from God to me.

For my husband, Darwin: I learn so much from you and love you more each day. Thank you for guiding me, not only spiritually but in all walks of life. I look forward to the adventures God has planned for us and our future together.

Thank you, Lord, for our times together at the window. I am excited to share the words You gave to me. For being with me always–I love You!

Table of Contents

1.	The Same	1
2.	Apple Blossoms	3
3.	Water Bowl and Turkeys	5
4.	Whiter Than Snow	9
5.	A Time to Cry	13
6.	Hard Worker and Provider	17
7.	Preparing the Ground	19
8.	Tonight's Cool Breeze	23
9.	Worth So Much More	27
10.	Playing Ball	31
11.	The Value of Antiques	35
12.	A Cry for Help	39
13.	The Effects of the Wind	41
14.	Tracker's Face	45
15.	Beauty in the Sky	47
16.	Children Wandering in the Woods	51
17.	Hummingbirds Fly?	53

18.	My Granddaughter in the Hammock	55
19.	Peeka's Garden	59
20.	Peeka Loves You This Much!	63
21.	Crowsnest Mountain	65
22.	Bubbles	69
23.	Like Father, Like Son	71
24.	Each One So Beautiful!	75
25.	Now Grown Men	79
26.	But I'm So Busy!	83
27.	Just a "Hi, I Love You!"	87
28.	My Friend	89
29.	Pa	91
30.	What If?	95
31.	Be on the Alert	99
32.	The Moon and Me	101
33.	Thanksgiving Day	105
34.	Bursting Through the Shadows	109
35.	Camouflaged?	111
36.	In the Hands of the Potter	113
37.	Abandon the Trike	115
38.	Ding -- Requires a Response	117
39.	Smoke is the Evidence of Fire	119
40.	Guarding, Guiding, Watching	121
41.	A Special Room Upstairs	125
42.	Moving Day	129
43.	It's a Girl!	133
44.	My New Window!	137
45.	Author's Note – Your Own Window	139

The Same

Jesus Christ is the same yesterday and today and forever.

Hebrews 13:8

As I look out of my kitchen window, a thought comes to my mind: If I close my eyes I can still see every detail of my backyard. The small red barn, the worn wooden fence, big and small pine trees surrounding our property, the round pen for our horses, a water trough, horseshoe pits, and even the rope swing; they all cry out for the safety I feel in the familiarity of this scene. I have often said, "If it works, don't fix it." I am not as good with change as I am with the familiar things in life. Oh, how content I can be in familiar surroundings. I now understand this may be the reason I spend so much time at my kitchen window. I have often thought it was because of the many dishes that needed washing. Now, I realize this is where I spend time looking, thinking, and talking with God. Not just talking to God, but waiting here at my window for His answers. He shows His faithfulness to me while meeting me at my window, showing His faithfulness in answering my cries of joy and sorrow at my window, and His faithfulness of revealing scripture through scenes from my window. He teaches me so many lessons while I look out of this small window. Today I realize how much I appreciate God's faithfulness. How much I enjoy His sameness, His familiarity, and His never changing love for me. God never changes; neither does His Word, His plans, His purposes, or His promises. He truly is the same yesterday, today, and forever.

Thank you, God, for my comfy home, for this beautiful property, and for this special window — a place where You and I spend so much time together.
See you here tomorrow God!

Apple Blossoms

I am the vine, you are the branches; he who abides in Me and I in him, he bears much fruit, for apart from Me you can do nothing.

John 15:5

As I look out of my kitchen window, I see the ripening fruit hanging like red bulbs on a Christmas tree. Apples, the tree is full of apples. I remember just a short time ago, looking out of this same window, as the tree was covered with delicate pink blossoms. Our small tree has been growing for quite a few years now. We have seen many seasons come and go together. This year its fruit is hanging from every limb.

Today, I am reminded of the scripture that describes Jesus as being the vine (John 15:5). The very real picture outside of my window is a visual of that verse for me. If I would have cut some of the branches, which were loaded with blossoms weeks ago, put them in a vase full of water, or if I would have replanted them, even in rich fertile soil, there would have been no apples today. The fruit would have never grown. The beautiful blossoms would have died. The branch would have eventually withered away. Spiritually, we are very similar. We must stay connected to the Vine (Jesus) in order to have eternal life and to produce spiritual fruit. We cannot do it alone. We cannot substitute any other environment for ourselves to grow, except to stay connected to Him. How easy it is to separate ourselves from the Lord and try to do things on our own. How easy it is to find other things to connect ourselves to as we live out life each day. But anything, other than staying connected to Christ, will only cause an unproductive life spiritually. The fruit that is produced is through Him and Him alone. The Bible says, "But the fruit of the Spirit is love, joy, peace, patience, kindness, goodness, faithfulness, gentleness, and self-control;" (Galatians 5:22-23).

Thank you, Lord, for these apples: we will enjoy eating them. Thank you too, for reminding me I must stay connected to you. I am looking forward to seeing the fruit that You will produce in my life as I do.

Water Bowl and Turkeys

Jesus answered and said to her, "Everyone who drinks of this water will thirst again; but whoever drinks of the water that I will give him shall never thirst; but the water that I will give him will become in him a well of water springing up to eternal life."
John 4:13-14

As I look out of my kitchen window, I witness the effects of today's high ninety-plus degree heat and intense sunlight. The backyard is turning brown, any little bit of grass we have is dying. There are grasshoppers everywhere. Then they come, by the tens and twenties, more than fifty wild turkeys are covering the parched field and finding their way into our backyard. They are looking for food, life sustaining food. What an amusing sight to watch the turkeys stretch their heads and necks to catch the grasshoppers as they spring off the ground. One lone turkey discovers my dog's water bowl, which was left in the middle of the yard last night. This bird seems so happy, almost smiling, as he takes a long drink from the small metal bowl and raises his head to swallow. He must have called to his friends, because within seconds there were two, three, up to fifteen at a time drinking this life sustaining water. They come for a cool drink in the high heat of the day, about 5:00 p.m.

    I can almost envision Jacob's well in the middle of town and the Samaritan woman. She came with her empty buckets at about 6:00 p.m. looking for physical life sustaining water. She came to the well all alone, an outcast among the women, not knowing that this was the place where she would meet Jesus. This was where she heard the precious words of life, "Everyone who drinks of this water will thirst again" (John 4:13). Jesus is the Living Water. Those who come to Him will have life eternal. The Samaritan woman found life and went to tell her friends. The picture I see looking out of my kitchen window reminds me of her and how we should be calling others to the same Living Water. The first turkey called today and about twenty-five of the more than fifty turkeys came for a drink. The other twenty-five or more just walked on by, still hot, still thirsty.

Within moments all the birds were gone, within moments the woman at the well would have been gone. What if Jesus had not taken the time to visit the well? What if He had not gone through Samaria, a place full of outcasts, half-breeds, people who did not acknowledge Him as Lord? He was weary, but not too tired to tell the good news to this one who had no knowledge of Him. Usually we only have but moments to make a difference in a person's life.

Help me Lord to be the one who brings others to You. Help me Lord to show them where You can be found. Though I may become weary I never want to be too tired to share Your story with one who does not know it. You are the only source of eternal life, the true Living Water.

Whiter Than Snow

Be gracious to me, O God, according to Your lovingkindness; according to the greatness of Your compassion blot out my transgressions. Wash me thoroughly from my iniquity and cleanse me from my sin. For I know my transgressions, and my sin is ever before me. Against You, You only, I have sinned.
Purify me with hyssop, and I shall be clean; wash me, and I shall be whiter than snow.

Psalms 51:1-4, 7

As I look out of my kitchen window, my backyard is completely blanketed in a soft, white covering. What just yesterday was brown and dirty, is now white and clean. Oh how I love the snow! It is falling ever so softly, like big white silver dollars floating down and then covering the ground. I look forward to this time every year, anticipating the beauty and quietness of a fresh snowfall. To wake up in the morning and see everything clean and white again is such a refreshing feeling for me. It is no wonder that God says in His scripture, "wash me and I will be whiter than snow" (Psalms 51:7). The white color is an amazing sight to behold. No dirt can be seen in it. It covers all that is muddy, messy, and dark. Even in the darkness of night, the reflection of the moon on the white snow illuminates our whole backyard, as if it were under a flood light. That is who Christ wants to be in me. The only way I can truly be clean is to be washed by His blood. I must realize that I am full of dirt, sin, and darkness; and I must turn my life over to Him. I did this when I was a teenage girl in the seclusion of my bedroom. A friend had shared the verse John 3:16 with me as we went through a carwash together. I later read the verse alone in my room and asked God to forgive me of my sin; I asked Him to be Lord of my life. At that very moment, I was made clean. At that very moment, if I had died, I would have gone to heaven to be with my Lord and Savior. But as I have grown in Christ, I realize just how much I continue to sin daily and the only way to be rid of that sin, dirt, and darkness is to confess it all to Him and ask for forgiveness. Jesus promises to forgive me and clean me up again. How much I love the feeling of forgiveness. How much I love the freshness of a clean start with Christ. Oh how I love to be whiter than snow! It is then that Christ can be illuminated through my life in the darkness of the world I live in.

Thank you, Lord, for washing me again today, as I come before You confessing my sin. Thank you for making me amazingly white, because without You I would be nothing but messy, dirty, and full of sin. This white snow blanketing my backyard is a vivid reminder of what You desire to do in my life!

A Time to Cry

There is an appointed time for everything. And there is a time for every event under heaven –
A time to give birth and a time to die; A time to plant and a time to uproot what is planted. A time to kill and a time to heal; A time to tear down and a time to build up. A time to weep and a time to laugh; A time to mourn and a time to dance.
                                        Ecclesiastes 3:1-4

As I look out of my kitchen window, tears are running down my cheeks. My husband and son are walking, for the last time, with a wonderful friend. His name is Buster. He is our horse, and what a friend he has been. He has carried my husband, family, friends and me through many adventures here in our backyard, along wooded trails, and through steep rugged mountains across Montana.

He has been loved by young and old. His big brown eyes have a way of drawing you to him for just a pat on his forehead or to stroke his mane. Buster has allowed so many to enjoy the wonder of a horseback ride without the fear that might normally overtake a person. He is gentle, curious, slow, even a blockhead sometimes. He has been a four-legged best friend for eleven years; and now we say our goodbyes. Disease has overtaken his body and we know he shouldn't suffer anymore. I say goodbye with such sorrow. But I also remember the many seasons full of great joy we had with him. The day we brought this brown and white paint horse home, he was only four years old. We were so excited with the hope of the future we would have with him. Little did we know how much he would change our lives. Little did we know the times of joy we would experience with this gentle horse named Buster. I am thankful to God for allowing us these times; still I am so conflicted in the goodbye. I know what the scripture says: "There is a time to give birth and a time to die" (Ecclesiastes 3:2), "There is a time to weep and a time to laugh" (Ecclesiastes 3:4). Where is the laughter today? Oh, I see Lord, this is the time to die, and this is the time for mourning. Help me Lord to look forward to tomorrow, to mourn today, but to laugh tomorrow.

These days do not just happen with the passing of a horse; they have happened throughout my life for many reasons. For the passing away of family and friends or the ending of friendships; for the loss of health in ones I love; for changes in my life that I have no control over and did not want to see happen. But I am drawn once again to the scripture which says, "There is an appointed time for everything" (Ecclesiastes 3:1). How wonderful is my God who teaches me, as I look out my kitchen window, of His appointed time for every event in my life.

Help me, Lord, not to take one minute, one day, one relationship for granted for I do not know what tomorrow holds, but I do know You hold and have appointed my tomorrow.

PS: Thank you, Lord, for all the joy we have had with Buster; what a blessing he has been to so many.

Hard Worker and Provider

Wives, be subject to your own husbands, as to the Lord. For the husband is the head of the wife, as Christ also is the head of the church, He Himself being the Savior of the body.
Ephesians 5:22-23

As I look out my kitchen window, I am smiling. Then it happens, my son walks up and asks with such curiosity, "What are you looking at mom?" Almost at the same time he asks the question he looks beyond my smile and out the window, sighs and walks away. I am admiring and smiling at my husband.

I am watching him in his well-worn, torn tan coveralls, work boots on, sweat beaded up on his forehead, and a shovel in hand, working hard and loving every minute of it. I am thankful to God for this man: for his work ethic, for his care and love for me, and for his love for God. I am thankful at this very moment for all he has provided for me throughout our years together. No, he is not perfect, but my heart is overflowing with gratitude and love for my husband and for God at the same time.

I know how much God loves me. I know how much God provides for me. I see His work in my life each and every day. I hear His voice speak to me in the good times and the bad; He truly is my comforter. God is my best friend who will never leave me nor forsake me. He is there when I am afraid. He is there when I just need to say, "Thank you." So, today, as I see the person God has joined me with, and who I will walk through life together with as best friends, I also realize, in human form, all that God wants to be for me if I will only let Him. I allow my husband the place and honor that he has in my life. I need to allow God the place and honor that He deserves in my life as well.

Lord, help me to love You and honor You more every day, forever. And thank You, for this hard working man and the wonderful gift of marriage.

Preparing the Ground

And He spoke many things to them in parables, saying, "Behold, the sower went out to sow; and as he sowed, some seeds fell beside the road, and the birds came and ate them up. Others fell on the rocky places, where they did not have much soil; and immediately they sprang up, because they had no depth of soil. But when the sun had risen, they were scorched; and because they had no root, they withered away. Others fell among the thorns, and the thorns came up and choked them out. And others fell on the good soil and yielded a crop, some a hundredfold, some sixty, and some thirty.

Matthew 13:3-8

As I look out of my kitchen window, I remember his frustration. Time and time again my husband has prepared the ground, sowed the seed, watered and waited only to be disappointed; the grass did not grow in our rocky field out back.

I think about the scripture, and see the reality of God's Word. I can almost visualize the different kinds of soil (heart) that could, or should, receive the seed (His Word) and allow it to grow. The seed in this scripture fell on four different types of soil. It fell beside the road, it fell on the hard and rocky soil, it fell among the thorns and weeds, and it fell on the good, rich soil. Each of these types of dirt reminds me of the hearts of people. Oh, how much God wants us to have a soft fertile heart where His word can take root and then to grow. Often the cares of our lives can easily turn our hearts to be hard, rocky, and so very full of the weeds that will choke out the Word, which God desires to grow in us.

I also see my husband as the pastor who loves people, and wants so much for their lives to be changed by God's living Word. I watch as he has worked to prepare the hearts of many people to receive God's Word. I see him, and many others, who care for people the same way a person cares for and prepares a field. Clearing, raking, and picking out the rocks: fertilizing, watering, and planting only to be disappointed when the weeds of life overtake their hearts. How much more God must be disappointed by the same thing. It becomes easy to see and understand the picture in God's Word describing the seed and soil.

As homeowners, we want the rocks and weeds out of our field so the grass seed can grow. As a person, do we really want the rocks and weeds of life out of our own hearts so as to let God's Word take root and grow? Both take hard work, effort, time, and attention. It doesn't just happen. I am reminded of the care that so many have taken for me throughout my life and their help in preparing my heart to be soft and fertile.

Thank you, Lord, for Your care and attention to my heart. Thank you, God, for reminding me today that I need to pull the weeds, and rocks out of my heart; for it to be soft and fertile to let your Word, not only take root, but also to grow in me.

Tonight's Cool Breeze

For you were called to freedom, brethren; only do not turn your freedom into an opportunity for the flesh, but through love serve one another.
Galatians 5:13

As I look out of my kitchen window, my heart is overflowing with joy. I see our backyard filled with children and adults of all ages: playing, laughing, and just plain enjoying one another. Tonight's cool breeze and the fresh air, encourage each one to relax and forget the busyness of the past week. There are groups playing, waiting, watching, and cheering as pairs compete in horseshoes. The large inflatable bounce house is filled with happy children just being kids. The horse is in the round pen, patiently waiting his next cowboy or cowgirl to mount and ride this trusty steed; each one sees him as their own pony. Children run into the woods in groups of two or more finding paths of adventure and building forts out in the young pine trees. All around the yard young and old are seated in lawn chairs, balancing plates filled with delicious food on their laps as they renew friendships and make new ones. The smile on their faces brings joy to my heart.

Then I see beyond the fun and there they are, the ones who are serving without anyone noticing. They are the three men who have been at the hot grill, cooking up hamburgers and hotdogs for over an hour. The one or two adults who have taken turns caring for the children entering and exiting the bounce house, making sure they are safe and playing fair while jumping inside. The adults and teenagers who are patiently teaching, lifting, walking, and encouraging the children as they mount, ride, and dismount their horse (their new friend). They are the few women who are already picking up the garbage, the older couple who get up from their chairs to sit by a person who has been sitting all alone, and the one man who wanders into the woods to check on the children who have been out of sight for a short while. They are the ones I see as true servants of God. They are serving because they love Him; they see the need before anyone asks.

I softly say, "Thank you God for showing me these special servants." I ask that I would remember, that I would be more willing, and that I would be looking for the small ways I can serve You with love; even in the midst of a fun evening of relaxation and fellowship. God, please burn this memory in my heart, that by love we should serve one another.

Worth So Much More

"For this reason I say to you, do not be worried about your life, as to what you will eat or what you will drink; nor for your body, as to what you will put on. Is not life more than food, and the body than clothing? Look at the birds of the air, that they do not sow, nor reap nor gather into barns, and yet your heavenly Father feeds them. Are you not worth much more than they?"

Matthew 6:25-26

As I look out of my kitchen window, I am amazed at the wildlife sanctuary I see. There they are again, but this time all at once: deer, rabbits, robins, turkeys, and horses. My husband and I have seen each of them before, as they enjoy the quietness of our backyard. The mother deer and her spotted fawns searching for the apples that have recently fallen from the tree, sneaking into the old barn for a taste of tender alfalfa hay, then running and playing through the young pine trees as they think nobody can see them. The rabbit that has become our friend over the years, he almost seems to watch for us as we come outside to throw him some special treats. We have named him Spot, and look forward to seeing him, too. I watch as a group of wild turkeys, at least fifty or more, who are there for only a few moments as they travel through, eating grasshoppers — how fun to watch them run and perch on the wooden fence, then in the blink of an eye, they are gone. The horses, who seem oblivious to all that is happening around them, but still eating and playing together as each horse is competing to be the head of the herd. I watch as a robin lands for just a few moments, searching the ground for one small morsel, then flies away as quickly as he came.

Oh, the amazing beauty of God's creation. Oh how He cares for each one and provides for each one in its own unique way. Then I remember how much He cares for me! How I am just one in this big world of many people who need His care, His provision, His love. How I am so much like this little rabbit just looking and waiting for His special treats. But then I realize; God is always providing for me, and not just when I am looking. I see the light green blades of grass and the leafy weeds that are there for this little friend in my yard, and I realize he has been provided for each day. Why do I look for more and not appreciate the small things God gives me? He has provided for the deer, the turkeys, the rabbits, the robins, and yes, even the horses right here within the small distance I can see. As I look out my kitchen window, I am reminded that I should not be anxious or worry; I am once again aware of the way God cares for me, too. I am worth so much to Him, my heavenly Father!

Thank you, God, for the simple things in life and for the great provisions that come only from You. Help me to truly appreciate what You have provided for me and to not be wanting more than You give me each and every day.

Playing Ball

Train up a child in the way he should go, Even when he is old he will not depart from it.
Proverbs 22:6

As I look out of my kitchen window, their energy becomes so engaging. There is such a competitive nature, between this father and his two sons. It is quite a comical sight. Yet, this is a moment that makes a mother proud. He is my middle child, only by ten minutes, as my first two are twins. He throws the ball with such speed to challenge his older son, and with such gentleness to encourage his younger one. He loves them both so very much. He knows how important it is to teach them at a level they can learn, yet provide opportunity for each son to succeed, even at this young age. They laugh, they run; they watch his every move wanting to be just like their dad. I think about how many times he will do the same thing over and over and over, until they get it right. Probably the same type of training for many years to come, but at different levels. This is playtime now, but there will come a day when each of these little guys will be out on a real ball field, playing in a real game, and then they will remember. All of this practice, repetition, encouragement, and even scolding, will someday be the tools they use while under pressure.

The Bible tells us that the way we train a child, while he is young, he will not depart from when he is old (Proverbs 22:6). This is not an absolute, but these teachings at a young age will be impressions that will become second nature as the child grows up. Of course we all have freedom to choose our own way, and not necessarily the way our parents taught us. Godly parents will teach their child from God's Word; then as the child grows, he or she will have to make his or her own choice of which way to go. This is the same for a parent who does not trust in the Lord, or His Word. A parent who teaches his child, in the formative years, dependence on anyone or anything other than God; impressions that will be second nature will not include the Heavenly Father when their child is making his or her own choices.

Oh, God, how You remind me of all the different training we put into our children, but the most important is not what happens on the ball field, it is what happens in their response to You. Training a child in the way he should go and when he is old he will not depart from it is all about You. We want our children to follow You, to trust You, to love You. Seeing faith lived out and practicing it over and over and over until we get it right is what pleases You. It would be a sight that makes You smile and makes You proud. Help us teach these little ones in such a way so that when they are old they will not depart from You! Thank you for my son and all the wonderful things he is teaching my grandchildren, especially while they are young.

The Value of Antiques

For we are His workmanship, created in Christ Jesus for good works, which God prepared beforehand so that we would walk in them.
                                              Ephesians 2:10

As I look out of my kitchen window, my attention is drawn to the rusted antique implements hanging as a decoration on our outside cedar wall. The common definition of antique is a collectible object such as a piece of furniture or work of art that has a high value because of its considerable age. But of what value do these objects hold, other than to look at them? They were used for farming, many, many years ago. We don't farm! We just look at them! Yes, they are interesting but really very useless.

Now I am getting older, but I never want to be useless for the Lord. I may take longer to do something, or ache when I do, *but please Lord, please don't just hang me on a wall – useless other than my presence in the room.* My mind is drawn to so many in the Bible used by God, even in their later years: Abraham lived to be 175 (was 75 when he was sent out to a land God would show him), Noah lived to be 950 years old (he was 600 when the floodwaters came upon the earth), and Methuselah was the oldest man ever, he lived to be 969 (grandfather to Noah). Wow, that is a lot of birthdays!

Now I am not feeling so old compared to these, as I am just in my fifties – well, almost finished with them, but still fifties. I see in God's Word that He uses all kinds of people, from all walks of life, and of all ages. That is great news. If I am willing to be used, He can and will, no matter what age I am. By the definition of an antique maybe God places a higher value on me because of my considerable age! Maybe I have more to offer than I know is possible. I am His workmanship, created to do good works. I need to just do them! Yes, "I can do all things through Him who strengthens me" (Philippians 4:13). It just may be slower.

Thank you, Father, for the many wonderful years of life You have blessed me with. Thank you, God, for creating me with a purpose and showing me the reality that it is not me doing anything but Christ working through me.

A Cry for Help

God is our refuge and strength, A very present help in trouble.

Psalm 46:1

As I look out of my kitchen window, my three youngest grandsons are playing in the snow. They are having so much fun sliding down a man-made snow hill and catching snowflakes on their noses and tongues as the pure white flakes gracefully fall from the sky. There he is, with the widest of eyes and the biggest smile that lights up his whole face the moment he notices me looking at him through the window. His expression is the same every time you see him. It almost reads: "Wow, it's you; I haven't seen you for so long and I love you!" He doesn't talk much yet but, that is what I see when he smiles at me. Within seconds his little hands turn red and cold as he falls into the wet snow. His gloves have slipped off and he is too young to put them back on by himself. His expression changes in the blink of an eye to: "Help me, pick me up, I'm cold, I love you!" I run out the door to rescue my little guy. There are tears streaming down his face and his hands hurt from the coldness of the day. We go inside by the fire and cuddle up together. I breathe warm air across his tiny hands as I cover his with mine. There it is again – his wonderful smile. He is okay now but my little one does not want to go out in the cold again.

How much I am reminded of my Father's love as I look onto His face: joy, excitement, love. Then it happens to me too, usually within seconds, something turns my otherwise wonderful day into a cold pain that I cannot get rid of on my own. God, help me I cry out, and He does. I feel safe in His arms, I feel the warmth of His love; and I even learn I'm not ready to go out into the cold again until He goes with me. My grandson and I bundle up and join the other two boys outside on the snow-hill to enjoy the beauty of creation, even in the cold.

Thank you, Lord, for my precious grandchildren, pure joy! Thank you too, for the warmth and safety I receive when I am wrapped in Your hands. I have nowhere else I would rather be today than watching these three boys and spending time just cuddling up with You – here at my kitchen window.

The Effects of the Wind

As a result, we are no longer to be children, tossed here and there by waves and carried about by every wind of doctrine, by the trickery of men, by craftiness in deceitful scheming; but speaking the truth in love, we are to grow up in all aspects into Him who is the head, even Christ.

Ephesians 4:14-15

As I look out of my kitchen window, I see the effects of the strong wind blowing outside. It almost seems as if I can see the wind, but I can't. I do see the leaves from the maple tree soaring upward to the sky, the brown sand twirling in the wind like a funnel while floating through the pasture, the plastic lawn chairs being blown over on their side, and the large pine trees swaying in rhythm to the unheard music. It all looks so orchestrated. It truly is an amazing sight. When it is all over, the destruction, debris, and mess will be there to clean up. This is such a visual picture of the scripture that tells us we should not be tossed about by every wind of doctrine. We should grow up. We are to be strong and steadfast in Christ, listen to and understand His Word; not be tricked by people and their deceitful schemes. As I look at the effects of this strong wind and see the destruction, I am also reminded of times in my own life where I was not planted, solid, strong in God's Word. It was those times that I was blown around by ideas and thoughts that seemed okay, but I knew were not of the Lord. It was those times when I remember the devastation that followed. Yes, I picked up the pieces the best I could and tried to clean up all that had fallen in around me. But did I really, or was some so broken they could never be fixed? Was some of the destruction in hurting those around me so great that even an apology for my actions did not take away the pain they experienced? I do see why God wants me to grow up and not be blown around anymore. It is not only about me, it is just as important for those I come in contact with every day. They need to see Christ in me. They need to know He is in total control of my life. To understand God's truth I must stay in His Word; just like the strong pines have deep roots.

The Effects Of The Wind

The tree may be blown by the wind, but it will not move; it will not allow the wind to change its position in our yard.

Lord, please help me to be strong in You more and more each day. I desire to be so firmly planted in Your Word that the storms of life will not move me. The storms will only confirm to me, and those around me, that my strength is in You.

Tracker's Face

Give thanks to the Lord, for His is good; For His lovingkindness is everlasting. Oh let Israel say, "His lovingkindness is everlasting." Oh let the house of Aaron say, "His lovingkindness is everlasting." Oh let those who fear the Lord say, "His lovingkindness is everlasting." From my distress I called upon the Lord; the Lord answered me and set me in a large place. The Lord is for me; I will not fear; What can man do to me?

Psalm 118:1-6

As I look out of my kitchen window, into a sea of blackness; I suddenly see a face looking back at me, it is full of fear. The darkness of night is everywhere outside and he wants to come into the house. He wants to be close to me. Heavy rain, thunder, and lightening have grown intense for a long while now and he doesn't like it. He is my dog, very big, so brave, so protective, so strong willed, but now so very afraid. Let me hide, please help me, let me not be alone; my dog's eyes seem to say to me. He has now climbed onto a chair to look at me, face to face, from the other side of this window.

How much I see my own reflection in this window. I seem so confident at times, so brave, so strong willed; and then the darkness comes. Then comes, the unfamiliar noises or bumps in the night. Oh how fearful I can become. It is almost as if I see my own reflection in the window, because I too want to run for protection so many times. Where do I go when I am afraid? Where do I go when darkness overpowers my life? Where do I go when storms are brewing all around me? So many times I run to the wrong places. But, the times I do go to my Savior, the One who loves me without fail, it is then that I find true relief and protection. I am comforted by God's promise when He says, "Do not fear, for I am with you" (Isaiah 41:10).

Thank you, Lord, for reminding me today that You are the One I can run to in all my times of fear. Thank you, Lord, for always being there when I need you.
(Okay Tracker, you can come inside. If anyone understands, it is me.)

Beauty in the Sky

"But you will receive power when the Holy Spirit has come upon you; and you shall be My witnesses both in Jerusalem, and in all Judea and Samaria, and even to the remotest part of the earth." And after He had said these things, He was lifted up while they were looking on, and a cloud received Him out of their sight. And as they were gazing intently into the sky while He was going, behold, two men in white clothing stood beside them. They also said, "Men of Galilee, why do you stand looking into the sky? This Jesus, who has been taken up from you into heaven, will come in just the same way as you have watched Him go into heaven."

Acts 1:8-11

As I look out of my kitchen window, florescent orange, pink, and yellow colors are erupting across our evening sky. This is not a common sight, as a small mountain normally hides the beauty of our Montana sunsets. This time, however, brilliant color is covering the whole sky and flowing over the top of the mountain into my range of sight. I love the beauty of a great sunset. I am not usually up or moving around in time to see the sunrise. But oh, the excitement I experience in watching the vibrant colors of a great sunset. This evening the clouds are moving through it as they change this amazing picture, moment by moment, right before my eyes. It all seems to happen so fast. If I look away for even a moment I may miss its magnificent beauty. I want this incredible color to stay forever!

The apostles must have felt the same way. It all happened so fast, as Jesus was lifted up, received by a cloud, and then out of their sight. These men did not want to miss a moment. They stood there gazing up, wanting Jesus to stay with them. They surely wanted to behold His beauty for just a little longer. But the angels came and gave hope for a future sunrise (no — Sonrise). Because this Jesus will come again in just the same way as He was taken. He will return from heaven and we will watch from earth. We will see the most amazing "Sonrise" at that time. Jesus promises to come again for those who love Him, for those who have given their lives to Him. He will then take us up to heaven to live with Him forever. Revelation 1:7 says, "Behold, He is coming with the clouds, and every eye will see Him, even those who pierced Him."

Thank you, Lord, for being my Savior. I look forward to Your return, Your Sonrise. Until then, I will enjoy every sunrise and sunset You send as a reminder of Your beauty and Your promised return.

Children Wandering in the Woods

Trust in the Lord with all your heart and do not lean on your own understanding. In all your ways acknowledge Him, and He will make your paths straight.
Proverbs 3:5-6

As I look out of my kitchen window, I can barely see their blue, gray, and red shirts through the trees. They have wandered deep into the forest behind our house. Well, really it is just a hundred yards or so away, but to these children today has become a great adventure to a faraway place. They build forts, they find bugs, they love to hide and chase each other until they get tired. The older one watches out for the younger three. They feel very safe because he is there with them and he knows the way back home. These four little boys left the security of their parents to follow this one who seems so confident and strong. They do not worry about what is around the corner because he has already traveled this well-worn path; truth-be-known, he probably cut it. Oh the fun and adventure of life seen through the innocent eyes of children. They don't worry about their meal; it will be there waiting for them. They don't care about their clothes; they know their parents will provide them. They really don't even consider tomorrow because today is so much fun!

Isn't that how it is with God? He said He would provide all our needs. Many of us were taught self reliance, independence on me and me alone. Which way do I go? Which path is best for me? Who do I trust? Jesus has already experienced everything we could ever imagine and is cutting a path for us to follow. Follow Him! Trust Him! He will never mislead us and God the Father is always watching our every move. Life is full of joy, adventure, and excitement; so let's enjoy today and let God take care of our tomorrow.

Thank you, Lord, for the adventures I experience each and every day. I choose to trust You for Your direction as You light my path, as You make it straight and easy to follow. Thank you for Your provision of food, clothing, shelter, and people who walk along side of me on my journeys in life. Yes, each person's path is different, but You are the same God who leads us through.

Hummingbirds Fly?

I can do all things through Him who strengthens me.
Philippians 4:13

As I look out of my kitchen window, I see it again, hovering in midair, as it is searching for nourishment from the nectar inside of the shiny glass feeder hanging off my back porch. It is beautiful, small, colorful, determined, and just plain amazing. The hummingbird's body is very unusual and because of its design I would think it should not be able to fly. It looks so different than other birds. I am in awe of its fascinating wing movement. This unique little bird can fly extremely fast, forwards and backwards, it can even hover over flowers to feed. This small bird with a bright red throat comes into my life with such eagerness and excitement. I stay at my window for a long time, wanting to see it's every movement. Suddenly, it darts away and is out of sight. It is only able to fly like it does because that is how God created it. I wait patiently for it to return. When it does I try hard to see this tiny bird's wings and to figure it out. Then I realize, God does not always want us to understand how something is able to work. He does want us to understand that we are able do things through His strength. I see today how He has made me a unique creature, too. I am only one, small person. I know that I should be more determined and eager in sharing Christ's love with others as I come in and out of their lives. I understand He has special jobs that He wants me to do and that these jobs can only be done because of His strength. I know there will be times when people will look at me, or I will see myself, and wonder how I can accomplish the task before me; it will be then I pray that others see Christ working and not me.

Thank you, Lord, for reminding me of where my strength comes from. Thank you for helping me to see myself as incapable without You, but with You, all things are possible.

My Granddaughter in the Hammock

"Come to Me, all who are weary and heavy-laden, and I will give your rest."
                                       Matthew 11:28

*A*s I look out of my kitchen window, I see her blond hair circling her face. She is young, she is beautiful inside and out; she is my granddaughter. Today has been a busy day full of activities; and now she is lying there cradled up in the hammock, covered with a blue checked flannel quilt and reading a book – well actually at this moment she is sleeping. My granddaughter loves to read. When at my house she especially loves to read outside; usually climbing up high to sit in her favorite pine tree, but this time in the comfort and quietness of the swaying hammock under the shade of our back porch. I know she is tired today. I saw it in her eyes right before she said, "Grandma, I'm going outside to read for a while." I have looked outside many times over the last half hour to see her curious eyes searching every page of the book held so tightly in her small hands. Now her eyes are closed, her breathing has become slower; her body resting. I learn from my granddaughter that we all need to find a place of rest. I know this is what God desires from me on so many of my busy days that are full of activities, only to realize that I just find something else to do. I search for peace and rest but I search in the wrong places. How easy it should be to know that when I am tired, burdened, busy, and weary I can go to a comfortable place to find real rest. The scripture is ringing in my ear: "Come to Me, all who are weary and heavy-laden, and I will give you rest" (Matthew 11:28). God is always waiting, anticipating that I come to Him when I am tired, busy or burdened. I see that rest is a choice I make and that the place I choose to go for true rest is my choice, too. The hammock was waiting today for my tired granddaughter, she made the right choice. She could have easily passed it by and found something else to do. She chose rest.

My Granddaughter In The Hammock

Thank you, Father, for my granddaughter; I love her so very much. Today has been a great day simply playing together. Thank you, Lord, for reminding me that You truly are the place for peace and rest and for reminding me that there is no other place I should go to find it.

Peeka's Garden

Seek the Lord while He may be found; call upon Him while He is near. Let the wicked forsake his way and the unrighteous man his thoughts; and let him return to the Lord, and He will have compassion on him, and to our God, for He will abundantly pardon. "For My thoughts, are not your thoughts, nor are your ways My ways," declares the Lord. "For as the heavens are higher than the earth, so are My ways higher than your ways and My thoughts than your thoughts. For as the rain and the snow come down from heaven, and do not return there without watering the earth and making it bear and sprout, and furnishing seed to the sower and bread to the eater; so will My word be which goes forth from My mouth; it will not return to Me empty, without accomplishing what I desire, and without succeeding in the matter for which I sent it. For you will go out with

As I Look Out of My Kitchen Window

joy and be led forth with peace; the mountains and the hills will break forth into shouts of joy before you, and all the trees of the field will clap their hands. Instead of the thorn bush the cypress will come up, and instead of the nettle the myrtle will come up, and it will be a memorial to the Lord, for an everlasting sign which will not be cut off."

Isaiah 55:6-13

As I look out of my kitchen window, I remember his words from yesterday, "Aren't these flowers beautiful?" exclaimed my oldest grandson. We were sitting together on the metal glider swing outside, both of us admiring a large patch of white flowers just beyond the worn wooden fence that lines the pasture. "Yes, they are! That's Peeka's garden!" I had responded, with a smile. (Peeka had been his name for me since he was very young, but now he usually just calls me Grandma!)

Today, as I look out of my kitchen window, I smile again remembering my grandson's comment. He and I both admired these flowers so very much. The same large patch of flowers that flowed across the small pasture like a sea covered in white foam others would have called them weeds. A field decorated with beautiful flowers was what we saw!

I am reminded of God's great desire for beauty. He has proven this over and over again in His amazing displays in creation. But, when I look at the small patch of ground which is my life, I know God's desire is for me to recognize and display beauty, His beauty! I can look at situations, trials, and struggles in my life with regret, remorse, even be unappreciative as if to say, "Why all the weeds?" When, really, God wants to show me His blessings even in the midst of those trials and struggles. Can there truly be a flower at the end of a weed and have an appreciation for the beauty of that flower? Can there truly be a blessing from God even in times of trials and struggles? Do I appreciate those blessings, even though they come in the form of what I myself and others see as weeds? Life is full of them, moments and days that are nothing more than weeds. They could distract me, discourage me, and even at times, choke the joy out of life. My God reminds me that only He can turn those same destructive weeds of life into a thing of beauty. His desire is for me to continually seek Him even in the midst of troubled days and to experience the joy He wants to provide. That which could destroy me, when turned over to Him, can become beautiful — even producing a flower to be seen and enjoyed by others.

As I Look Out of My Kitchen Window

Thank you, Lord, for this large patch of flowers. Thank you for reminding me that You truly desire more for my life. You desire more than the weeds, that can and do, grow so easily. You desire beauty from my life! I am thankful for the splendor of Your amazing creation, some of which is seen right here from my kitchen window; even in the midst of weeds!

Peeka Loves You This Much!

"For God so loved the world, that He gave His only begotten Son, that whoever believes in Him shall not perish, but have eternal life."

John 3:16

As I look out of my kitchen window, I almost get lost in his captivating smile. I am drawn to the excitement displayed on this little face as he sprays everything in sight with the water nozzle. His small body takes all of its strength to hold and pull the long line of hose. Then his curious eyes meet my eyes looking back at him through this window. He is my grandson, I am Peeka to him. He wants me to watch his every move. He wants to show me all of his amazing accomplishments. He wants to share this moment with me, the thrill of spraying water. It seems so small, but I am overcome with joy and love for him. Then I motion to him our secret little gesture. I show him my finger and thumb held about an inch apart, which means Peeka loves you this much. His reply is always to hold his arms out as wide as possible, shaking his head with the response: "No Peeka, this much, as big as the whole wide world." I know there are many people who show this same loving gesture to their children and grandchildren.

Today I am reminded of my Father, my Heavenly Father. How often I look to see if He is watching me and approving of what I am doing. How I want to share my moments, my accomplishments, with Him. When I think of the scripture that says God loved me so much that He sent His only Son (John 3:16), I realize, how Jesus stretched out His arms as wide as they would go to be nailed on the cross and die for my sin, for my salvation. I realize how often I think God loves me just a little bit, but really, He loves me bigger than the whole-wide-world. He showed me by His arms stretched out wide on the cross.

Thank you, Lord, for giving Your Son who died on the cross so I can spend eternity with You in heaven. Not just for me, but for anyone who is willing to confess their sin and accept Him as Lord and Savior. I also appreciate how You are always watching me, whatever I do and wherever I go.

CROWSNEST MOUNTAIN

I will lift up my eyes to the mountains; from where shall my help come? My help comes from the Lord, Who made heaven and earth.
                              Psalm 121:1-2

I awake in the middle of the night to such darkness all around me. I try to look out of my kitchen window but the night is so black that I cannot see anything beyond the clear glass before me. The vast darkness I am experiencing is not only due to the absence of the moon, but also an immense darkness in the loneliness of tonight. It has been a long few weeks and life has not turned out as I had planned. Where are You, God? Why God? These questions keep shouting in my head as I try to figure out this life and all of its new trials. My thoughts take me back to a drive I took not long ago, as I was returning home to Montana from Canada. On that long drive I looked for, cried out to, and heard from God. It was an awesome revelation as I drove past Crowsnest Mountain. This is what I wrote down that memorable day:

> It was a sunny day as I was driving through Canada and I once again drove by Crowsnest Pass Mountain. I remember meeting this mountain twenty one years ago; I was in awe of its beauty and majesty. I have driven past this familiar mountain many times throughout the years. Many of the days were like today, sunny and easy to see the amazing beauty of this mountain. Some of the days were foggy and I could barely see the outline of the mountain, sometimes it was partially covered by thick white clouds and I could only see the glory of its majestic peak. Other times I drove by in the darkness of night and it seemed as though the mountain was not even there at all. This amazing mountain has never moved, I just couldn't see it or I couldn't see it clearly.

I met Jesus many years ago. I was awed by His beauty and majesty. I trusted Him to be my Lord and Savior. Many of my days were sunny, clear, bright, and easy to see Jesus and all that He has done for me. But, throughout my life there have been days filled with fog or darkness, just like the darkness of night, where I was not able to see Him clearly or even see Him at all. Yet, He was still there – solid, firm in all of His majesty and glory. He has never moved – He is the same yesterday, today, and forever.

Just like this majestic mountain that has stood through the storms of life and has never moved, so is my Lord; He has never moved. I am the one who has the problem seeing and trusting. I am the one who allows the trials of life which act as fog or darkness to separate me. I need to remember that whether on bright sunny days, or in the very darkest times of life, my God is always there! I will put my trust in the one who never changes!

January 2013

So, even tonight I remember. Though the night is dark and lonely, I may feel like God is not here, but He is. I choose to remember that He never changes or moves!

Thank you, Lord, for Your steadfastness; for Your love that endures forever! I will go to sleep now with the confident assurance that You are with me. Thank you for never changing or moving, just like the mountains all around me, and the beautiful reminder that my help truly, and only, comes from You!

Bubbles

Yet you do not know what your life will be like tomorrow. You are just a vapor that appears for a little while and then vanishes away.
James 4:14

𝓑ubbles are floating past, as I look out of my kitchen window! I turn to see my young grandson and his mother sitting side by side on the stairs of our deck, laughing as they blow bubbles together. His face is full of wonder and excitement and hers is full of joy and pride. What a beautiful picture for a grandmother to hold in her heart — the love of family. The simple joy of laughter is something we too often take for granted. This day has been a peaceful day, as we do not have to do anything, just be together. I laugh again, one of the bubbles pops as it lands on my grandson's tiny round face. His look of surprise is priceless. His sweet smile flows all the way through his great big eyes and his laughter is so contagious.

Help me to remember the joy and love that I share with you as my Heavenly Father. As I look at the world around me, I too am full of wonder and excitement; and You look at me with joy and pride. The bubbles of my life, joy and amazement over the little things, are so easy to miss and so easy to let float by without notice. Then, just like these bubbles my precious grandson is enjoying, the moments of life are gone like a vapor in a breeze. It is as if time pops right before my face. My desire is to appreciate, to enjoy, and to laugh at the big and small moments of my life. Moments and time are lovely gifts from You.

Thank you, Lord, for the gifts You have given to me: husband, children, and grandchildren. And life counted by special moments, full of just blowing bubbles.

Like Father, Like Son

I will open my mouth in a parable; I will utter dark sayings of old, which we have heard and known, and our fathers have told us. We will not conceal them from their children, but tell to the generation to come the praises of the Lord, and His strength and His wondrous works that He has done. For He established a testimony in Jacob and appointed a law in Israel, which He commanded our fathers that they should teach them to their children, that the generation to come might know, even the children yet to be born, that they may arise and tell them to their children, that they should put their confidence in God and not forget the works of God, but keep His commandments.

Psalm 78:2-7

As I Look Out of My Kitchen Window

As I look out of my kitchen window, he is standing there with his father. His father is my youngest son, tall with dark hair and dark eyes. He looks so much like my husband when he was that age; oh how much these three look alike. Father and son are positioning a child's bow against my grandson's small body: stand, aim, and shoot. Father teaching son, just as his father had taught him so many years ago. The feathered arrow hits the cardboard target! My young grandson shouts, turns, and smiles at his father. They are both so very proud of this three year olds accomplishment. They embrace as they look into each other's eyes, eyes full of excitement and pride. The two are one, as they pick up the bow for another attempt at hitting the bull's eye.

I am reminded that in the scripture we are commanded to aim at the bull's eye and strive not to miss the mark; to do all that God has asked of us. This is something to be taught from generation to generation. Sin, missing the mark, is so easy and so natural. So natural that nobody has to teach us to sin, it is our human nature. We do, however, need to be taught God's Word and of His great love for us. We do need to be taught obedience, both to our parents and to our Heavenly Father. How will this happen if fathers and mothers do not take the time to teach God's truth to their children? According to scripture, it is our responsibility to teach God's Word to our children: as we lay down, as we rise up, as we walk by the wayside. We are to write it down for them (Deuteronomy 6). My excited grandson would not have learned to shoot this bow and arrow at such an early age if his father had not spent the time with him. His father is sharing something he loves with someone he loves, and he has learned all of this from his father who loves him. How beautiful a picture of our Heavenly Father Who loves us, He has revealed this love to our fathers and they taught it to us. I see my beautiful grandson, who looks so much like his father, (my son) and he looks so much like his father (my husband). I see their love for archery, which has now been passed down to a third generation. I also see men who look like their Heavenly Father, and because of their great love for Him, they teach His Truth to their sons. Three generations looking like their father on earth and their Father in heaven.

Thank you, Lord, for men who love You and are willing to teach of Your love to the generations that follow.

Each One So Beautiful!

An excellent wife, who can find? For her worth is far above jewels.
Proverbs 31:10

*A*s I look out of my kitchen window, I cannot help but admire their beauty; each one so different, each one my daughter-in-law. I love them so much and appreciate the love they have for my sons and grandchildren. They are young, Lord; they have so much life ahead of them. Will it be a life that is full of Your presence and peace? Not a life without trouble and trials, because we both know that cannot be, but Lord I do pray that my girls learn to lean on You when tough times come. They are smiling right now, as they talk with each other. Children, husbands, dogs, and horses are all around; but they are talking as if no one else is there. They are family. Two of my girls were raised here in this little town and I had the privilege of watching them grow up. As a school secretary, I was a part of their lives in their younger years. One I met as an adult. I have spent time with her family and recognize the similarity in our backgrounds. I feel as though our lives were always one. I was encouraged many years ago, when we lived in Alabama, by another young mother; to pray for my sons and to also pray for their future wives. My boys were only young children at that time. However, she reminded me there was a very special little girl being raised, right then, and would someday become their wife. She would bring all of her life experiences, good and bad, to the marriage. Would she be raised in a Christian home or not? Would she know the love of You as her Heavenly Father or not? So, I did; I prayed for many years. I did not pray daily, like I should have, but I did pray regularly for these girls who I did not even know. Now, here they are, not little girls anymore but beautiful women all grown up; and I had been a part of their growing up by praying for them throughout the years. They never knew how much I loved them! They never knew how I held them in my heart before my eyes ever looked upon their face.

Each One So Beautiful!

God, You are like that. You loved us before we knew You. You watch us as we grow. Your great desire is that someday we would accept You as Lord and Savior and that we would become your children.

Thank you, Lord, for Your great love for me. Thank you for giving these beautiful girls as a precious gift to my sons, and to my husband and to me!

Now Grown Men

Behold, children are a gift of the Lord, the fruit of the womb is a reward. Like arrows in the hand of a warrior, so are the children of one's youth. How blessed is the man whose quiver is full of them; they will not be ashamed when they speak with their enemies in the gate.
Psalm 127:3-5

As I look out of my kitchen window, I hear their voices coming from over my left shoulder. I am amazed at such strong and deep voices from these three men sitting in the dining room. Wasn't it just yesterday that they were teenagers at this same table, in this same room? No, it's been years (fifteen or more) and I just don't know where the time has gone; the days and the years have evaporated like a puff of smoke before my eyes. My sons have grown up to be such fine men, hardworking, love the outdoors, and play as hard as they work. These are men who love their families and love the Lord. I am so proud of each one of them. My heart is full of thankfulness for this moment. It is hard to explain the feelings of joy as I look at the smiles on their faces, their wives faces, and my grandchildren's faces, too. Loving our children is such a natural thing. To have invested a lifetime in them: from birth to graduation, diapers to blue jeans, colic to late-night phone calls; nurturing, training, feeding, and loving — now reaping the rewards! This is what we hoped and prayed for. Not expecting perfection, as we may not always like the things they do, but our love never fails. It is no different when I think of my heavenly Father. His love for me is never-failing! I'm sure there are even times when He hears my voice and just smiles because He loves me so much! I am a child of God and nothing can change that. I can ignore Him, but He is still my Father. I can disappoint Him, but He will still love me. I guess it is just easier to see and understand my relationship with God as I watch my own sons and remember my great love for them. Never ending!

Help me, Lord, to remember this special moment. I appreciate the gift You gave me at the moment

of my sons' births. I also thank You for the many moments that we have shared since then and will not take any for granted. These children of mine, though now grown men, are precious in my sight and Yours.

But I'm So Busy!

Now as they were traveling along, He entered a village; and a woman named Martha welcomed Him into her home. She had a sister called Mary, who was seated at the Lord's feet, listening to His word. But Martha was distracted with all her preparations; and she came up to Him and said, "Lord, do You not care that my sister has left me to do all the serving alone? Then tell her to help me." But the Lord answered and said to her, "Martha, Martha, you are worried and bothered about so many things; but only one thing is necessary, for Mary has chosen the good part, which shall not be taken away from her."
Luke 10:38-42

As I look out of my kitchen window, the sun is so amazingly bright today; it draws my attention outside. It is almost calling me: "Come, sit in the swing under the tree, feel my warmth, rest a while in my light." Then all of a sudden my eyes see it, a dirty spot on the window; oh no, I need to wipe it off! As I reach under the sink for window cleaner, I notice the overflowing garbage needs to be taken out. But I have dishes to wash, a table to set, and dinner to cook because company is coming over soon. My heart is racing, my mind is wondering, "What do I do first?" I become so anxious and troubled. I do enjoy cooking, cleaning, and serving but so much of the time I become preoccupied while doing it. Preoccupied by the work and forget the reason —love.

I remember the words of Jesus as He spoke to a similar woman in the Bible. She too was so busy trying to prepare for company; she was preparing for Jesus Himself. Her name was Martha, and she became so distracted in all of the preparation that she didn't have time for the One that was most important, the One she was preparing for, the One she loved. However, her sister Mary was sitting at Jesus' feet. She was listening and learning, not out of slothfulness, but out of love. Martha complained about her sister to Jesus. Did she truly want help or was she just grumbling? He told Martha that Mary had chosen the better thing!

But I'm So Busy!

I can get so distracted. I know what or who should be most important, but I allow the little things to pull me away, to worry me, to distract me. Even now, as I am looking out of my window thanking God for this sunshine, praising Him for all He has given me, yet a speck on my window or the garbage in my kitchen pulls me away from the true Son. Yes, we have a responsibility to work and to clean, but spending time at Jesus' feet is more important than anything else we do!

Help me, Lord, I am so much like Martha and yet I desire to have a Mary's heart. I desire to spend time with You; sitting, learning, resting, and just enjoying the warmth of Your love! Ok, I will go out to the swing for a few minutes and just be with You, everything else can wait — Thank You!

Just a "Hi, I Love You!"

Because you are sons, God has sent forth the Spirit of His Son into our hearts, crying, "Abba! Father!" Therefore you are no longer a slave, but a son; and if a son, then an heir through God.
Galatians 4:6-7

As I look out of my kitchen window, the silence in the room is abruptly pierced by the familiar ringtone of my phone. I look at the display to see it is my oldest son calling. His hello is with such enthusiasm; his tone is full of joy as he tells me about his day and also the plans for his tomorrow. He did not call for any reason except to talk. Oh how these kinds of phone calls cheer a mother's heart, my heart. This time I only ask a few questions as he goes from one subject to another; mostly I just listen. I love to hear about his day, his wife, his job, and his love for the Lord. He has committed his life to Jesus, and anyone who knows him can see it clearly. It's in his voice inflection, in the words he chooses, and the subjects that are dear to his heart. I am so very proud of him. I am so thankful for the godly man he is. Then, as quick as the conversation began, he says, "I've got to take this business call, mom. Love you, bye." We hang up and I think how nice it was to hear from him, to hear him call me mom. I so love to hear the word "mom"; it's an endearing name, allowed to be used by one's own child. I often smile in the store when I hear a little child, who feels lost, holler, "Mom!" In the scripture the word Abba is used by a son calling out to his father, daddy. As children of God, we have a relationship and a direct line of communication with Him, our heavenly Father.

But what about me, do I call God just to talk? Do I call with excitement, enthusiasm, just to tell Him about my day and that I love Him? Not as often as I should. Usually, it goes more like this, "Hello God, I need you, help me, show me." I know God is not disappointed to hear from me anytime that I call, but I wonder if sometimes He would just like to hear about my day, my joys, and that I truly love Him.

I think I will try it right now, "Hey God, it's me. I just want You to know what a great day I had. I love You."

MY FRIEND

By this the love of God was manifested in us, that God has sent His only begotten Son into the world so that we might live through Him. In this is love, not that we loved God, but that He loved us and sent His Son to be the propitiation for our sins. Beloved, if God so loved us, we also ought to love one another.
1 John 4:9-11

As I look out of my kitchen window, I am tired and laboring to breathe. I am sick again. As a child, I was exposed to so much second hand smoke that my lungs are now weak. I know I won't be up for very long but I just need to do something, anything except sit on the couch, again! I hear a car as it comes up my gravel driveway; it is my friend and she has brought me dinner and something to drink. She knows how I feel even though she does not deal with the same health problem. But a true friend she is. We have experienced much of life together. She has been there through times of celebrations and encouraging me through times of sorrow or stress. We take walks, talk, and laugh. How much I appreciate her caring heart and love for me. Sometimes it is just a phone call, or she wants to know that I made it home safely from a long drive. Other times we share dreams, we pray for each other and for our families. We have served alongside each other for many years at church. I will never take her tenderness and friendship for granted. Throughout my life I have had many caring people all around me. Some became close friends, so close we were almost like family to one another. True friends are such a beautiful gift from God. I have been blessed with many.

I have another friend, and His name is Jesus. He comes to me when I am sick or tired, and when life is full of joy or sorrow. We walk together, talk together. I choose to serve Him; and my desire is to be a blessing to Him. He is a friend who loves me always; One who never fails.

Thank you, Lord, for my special friend; please bless her today as she is such a blessing to me.

PA

But as many as received Him, to them He gave the right to become children of God, even to those who believe in His name, who were born, not of blood nor of the will of the flesh nor of the will of man, but of God.
John 1:12-13

As I look out of my kitchen window, he is sitting under the shade tree; but this time with a different look on his face. Normally, he is full of smiles or mischief, but age and health are taking a toll on his body. There are times that he repeats himself, the same story over and over. We just nod and say, "Ok Pa." He has been more of a father to me than my own. I met him when I went to their house for dinner my senior year of high school. I even spilled my glass of iced tea at the table that night, but he did not get upset with me. Not a response I was use to experiencing. He loved me even when I made mistakes. I will never forget his strong engulfing hugs. I was not born into his family but I took his last name, and truly became his child, when I married his son, I know I became his favorite daughter-in-law (ok, so all his other children were girls). But I did know that he loved me — through all these years of doing family, good or bad, he loved me. He did not always agree with me, and that was ok, because I respected him and tried to learn from him. Now, today, at this moment he looks so lost. We have had a wonderful time this week with family all around, meals together, and stories told. He is tired and I think he is a little forgetful right now. I will leave my kitchen and just sit with him. These are precious moments and I will always appreciate them.

I also have a heavenly Father that loves me. He never changes, will never grow old or forgetful. He always enjoys my company. I am His daughter, nothing I do will ever take that away. I know this man I am sitting with is a gift from God; some tangible way that I can know who God the Father is and how much He loves me.

Pa

Thank you, Lord, for my father-in-law and for the many years that he has been there for me and loved me when I was not very lovely. Thank You for giving me a place, as a daughter, in this family here on earth and the right to be called Your daughter, too.

WHAT IF?

If it is disagreeable in your sight to serve the Lord, choose for yourselves today whom you will serve; whether the gods which your fathers served which were beyond the River, or the gods of the Amorites in whose land you are living; but as for me and my house, we will serve the Lord.

Joshua 24:15

As I look out of my kitchen window, I remember the words like they were spoken moments ago. But it was not, it has been months, or was it years now. Fortunately, I do not remember the date or the circumstance; however I distinctly recall the place and the voice. I was driving to work and praying so hard about something, crying out to God for an answer. Well, He answered. It was not an audible voice but it was very clear: "Will you trust Me and serve Me?" I responded, "Yes Lord, you know I will." He replied, "What if I take your job, your house, your health, your friends, your children, and your husband?" After each request I committed myself to Him — no matter what!! It was a devastating conversation with God, but at the same time a revealing of my love for Him. I know He can take anything away from me that He chooses but the question still remains, will I continue to choose Him, to trust Him, to serve Him. My answer that day was yes, and still is. I will not say that is was easy, actually it was very scary because I wondered what that day would hold! I pass by that curve in the road every time I drive into town. I feel at times I should put a marker there, just for me, as a reminder of my commitment to God — no matter what, I will trust and serve You!

I think of the many people in the Bible who never turned back — no matter what. They faced famine, war, ridicule, beatings, shipwrecks, and even death; but they continued to trust and serve God — no matter what. Stories of faithful men and women do not end with the Bible.

My life may be full of changes and challenges, but the one constant is God and His love for me! I made the choice many years ago, as for me and my house we will serve the Lord. I chose to put away other gods, over and over again throughout my life. Many times the choice was an easy one. Many times it was not. I can say without a shadow of a doubt, choosing God is always best — no matter what!

Thank you, Lord, for reminding me that it is always my choice. You do not force me to love or serve You. If so, it would not be love. Yes Lord, I choose You.

BE ON THE ALERT

Be of sober spirit, be on the alert. Your adversary, the devil, prowls around like a roaring lion, seeking someone to devour.
1 Peter 5:8

As I look out of my kitchen window, the sun is shining so bright. There is no one in the yard and no animals are around. It all seems as still as a landscape picture hanging on a wall, but it is not. There is movement, ever so slight, yet still there is movement. It looks like hundreds of raindrops (without any rain in the sky) falling from the limbs of the small maple tree just yards from my window. I hurry outside to examine this movement up close. Even as I stand next to the tree I don't know what they are. A closer look and I can see, tiny worms sliding down a silk like thread by the hundreds from our frail tree. Army worms! They are army worms, and if left unchecked they will destroy what we have planted and planned on for future shade. They work in unity as they follow each other, covering and devouring this tree right before me. These insects are so very small, but so very powerful. Ouch, sin works the same way; small, sometimes unnoticed until it multiplies itself and never giving up until it covers what is good, destroying all hope, and even any plans for the future. Stop it — quick — get the bug spray and get rid of these worms.

We can do the same with all those small sins that we allow to slide into our life. Stop it — quick — go away Satan! Jesus I need You to fight the enemy's army for me. Just as this beautiful living tree cannot remove the worms itself; we are helpless without the protection of Jesus. We are God's beautiful living creation and need only to call on His name, ask for forgiveness of sin, and Satan will be defeated. Good News!

The bad news is — keep watching — the worms (and sin) will show up again. However, this time we can be ready! Bug spray in one hand and a Bible in the other.

Thank you, Lord, for Your protection. I know the devil is prowling around looking to attack me when I least expect it. Help me to keep my mind on You and to always be on the alert.

The Moon and Me

In the beginning God created the heavens and the earth.

Genesis 1:1

Then God said, "Let Us make man in Our image, according to Our likeness; and let them rule over the fish of the sea and over the birds of the sky and over the cattle and over all the earth, and over every creeping thing that creeps on the earth." God created man in His own image, in the image of God He created him; male and female He created them.

Genesis 1:26-27

As I look out of my kitchen window, the aroma of coffee brewing invites me to begin a treasured morning routine. With heavy eyelids, I carefully fill my snowman mug and head to the living room where I will begin my day reading God's Word. Gazing out the large front window, my attention is drawn to a steel blue sky shining through the darkness; a black silhouette of pine trees almost resembling a frame around a bright crescent moon as it rises. All is still as this sleepy morning breaks. The day is beginning with such quietness and peace. Songs on the radio, a cup of hot coffee warms my hand, a fireplace at full blaze, my softest blanket, and a comfy recliner. I come to this place most mornings to read. This is one of my favorite places where I meet God in the morning, or other times throughout the day to explore His Word. It's wonderful to have my days begin like this; no pressure, no distraction, and today the added beauty from the light of this bright moon. My mother loved the beauty of God's creation. She loved people, just as they were, not expecting anything from anyone. I will always appreciate her generosity and her teaching me to love others. I am reminded of a little rhyme she would tell me when I was young: 'I see the moon and the moon sees me, God made the moon and God made me!'[1] Such an amazing truth in a simple song, but it is also a great reminder as I look up to the heavens. Today, I look just because of its beauty and I am in awe of God's creation. He is the artist painting this scene right here in front of me. He placed the moon in the sky for a purpose. He created me and placed me here for a purpose, too.

Please Lord, show me how You want to use me today, and that others would acknowledge You when they see Your creation – me! Yes, even me, made in Your image with a purpose. You made the moon and You made me!

THANKSGIVING DAY

Rejoice always; pray without ceasing; in everything give thanks; for this is God's will for you in Christ Jesus.

1 Thessalonians 5:16-18

As I look out of my kitchen window, I pause. All of my senses are on high alert, celebrating the blending of smells, fresh baked pumpkin pies, homemade granny rolls, and a roasted turkey sprinkled generously with butter and garlic. My kitchen tile is cool under my bare feet but the air is warm, almost hot, from the long hours opening and closing the oven door and stirring pots full of mashed potatoes and gravy on top of the stove. I love the smells of Thanksgiving dinner. It never ceases to amaze me that our country recognizes this day as a national holiday but so many people do not know Who to thank. Why Lord, can they not see You in the simple or great moments of life?

As I move today, back and forth, to my sink and looking out of this window I thank You Lord for my husband, sons, daughters-in-law, grandchildren, extended family, and friends. I thank You for my church, for my health, job, house, vehicles, pets; and even for this sort of red colored tile on my kitchen floor — 1 love its look and feel. I thank You for my guys as they have these moments today to just be together hunting. I thank You for my dishwasher that I have already run two or three times today, saving my hands from all the grimy water. Thank You, Lord, for the table, china hutch, and buffet that was lovingly given to me by my precious mother-in-law. She provided my family with years of a great setting as many meals were shared on this antique table, the same one she raised her own children on. I thank You for this godly woman, her love for You and for me, and for so much that she taught me about life. As I am putting together the cornbread dressing, reading from her hand written recipe, I realize I have prepared this same dish the same way every Thanksgiving since she gave it to me. And every year at this time, as many other times throughout the year, I am so thankful for her!

As I present my list of thanksgiving before You God, I am also praying that our nation would realize Who You are. People, individuals, would come to a saving faith in You. Then they would know Who to thank on this special day and every day. Yes, in everything we are to give thanks, to You!

Bursting Through the Shadows

Some trust in chariots and some in horses, but we trust in the name of the Lord our God.
Psalm 20:7 NIV

As I look out of my kitchen window, two large forms come bursting through the shadows of the young, snow covered pines; clouds of powdered snow rising around each one. With speed and strength, I can almost hear their hoofs pounding the ground, as if someone was beating a rhythm on an African drum. Nostrils flared wide, I see their breath shooting out like steam from a tea kettle in this cold morning air. Our two horses are playfully chasing each other through the woods, across the small field, around the corner of the house into the front pasture; then repeating the same path again. Over and over again! I watch with admiration at their beauty, strong bodies, and great speed. These horses are our pets, just for pleasure. In times past, animals just like these were used for work and transportation. They pulled plows and wagons, carried families across the plains, and soldiers into battle. Horses back then were not valued as much for pleasure as they were trusted for life itself. There was such a dependence on them.

I am drawn to the scripture — 'Some trust in chariots or horses, we will trust in the Lord God' (Psalm 20:7). Even though I do not live in an era that I need to have such a trust in horses, I can see where it has come from, as I observe their muscular bodies in this powerful race before me.

More often than not I put my trust in modern day transportation, cars and trucks, and machines or computers that make my everyday life's work more manageable; even armies that protect me daily (though I never see them). Why do I trust this which has not created me or that which never will sustain me? Why do I trust things that will make my life simpler and not the One Who gave life to me? I agree with the scripture, I will choose to trust God above anyone or anything, in spite of their great strength.

Thank You, Lord, for this scene before me; for the snow, trees, and strong racing horses. Thank You for reminding me where my trust must be placed – in You.

Camouflaged?

I have given them Your word; and the world has hated them, because they are not of the world, even as I am not of the world. I do not ask You to take them out of the world, but to keep them from the evil one. They are not of the world, even as I am not of the world.

John 17:14-16

As I look out of my kitchen window, a tiny white spot behind the dried-up brown brush reveals a young fawn. She is laying just a few yards away, unseen until I noticed a bright patch of white and then a twitch of her tiny ear. I have already walked by three or four times without distinguishing her camouflaged body from the weeds. She knows she is safe here. No one will trouble her. The yard gives her plenty of room to run and to play, shade trees for a cool rest, leaves, hay and water to nourish, and so many places to hide.

I feel like this young one at times; vulnerable and in need of a refuge from all the troubles of life that seem to linger around every dark corner and startle me without notice. A safe place for me to dwell is what I long for. As a child of the King I know that He provides, not only a home for me in heaven, but safety with Him here on earth. I also understand that He does not want His children to hide, to be camouflaged, and blend in with a world that does not know Him. We do live in the world, but should not look like the world. We are to be seen as the beautiful creation uniquely designed by Him; and taking every opportunity to tell others about Him. Yes, God is a place of safety and refuge like my yard is for this frail fawn. He also provides the courage for me to step out as He goes with me to do the work He has created me for and sent me to do.

Thank you, Lord, for all the safe places You have provided for me. I will remember that when I venture out into this sometimes scary world — You are with me, even sending me. I understand that I am to be different than the world around me and not to just blend in, or to be camouflaged. I need to look more like You as I go about my daily routine.

IN THE HANDS OF
THE POTTER

So I went down to the potter's house, and I saw him working at the wheel. But the pot he was shaping from the clay was marred in his hands; so the potter formed it into another pot, shaping it as seemed best to him.
Jeremiah 18:3-4 (NIV)

As I look out of my kitchen window, sunlight reflects a glow off of the cobalt blue clay pot containing purple pansies, in full bloom. It's hard for me to decide today which is prettier, the pot or its contents. Normally, plants have a way of dying while in my care. Somehow this one has made it. Almost anyone who knows me knows my love for pottery. Some would even say an addiction. When traveling, I bring home souvenirs as often as possible in the form of pottery. Family and friends have given gifts of love to me in the form of pottery. Collections of various colors, shapes, and sizes are scattered throughout my house. It is no wonder the verse in the Bible which describes God as the potter and me as the clay (Isaiah 64:8) is so dear to me. The pot does not tell the potter how it should be shaped or used. I should be thankful for the way God has individually created me, with a special purpose chosen only by Him. How often I complain to You Lord, desiring something different from You in my looks, or in my serving. But today I am reminded once again, as I glance at all the pottery around me, each one is so unique. Some are large and colorful, like the one I am admiring full of beautiful flowers blossoming in the right season. Some are small, brown and tan like the one hanging from my mug tree, used for hot coffee, tea, or cocoa. Many pieces of pottery of individual shapes, sizes, colors, and uses are within my area of sight. All were created for a specific use, not by its own choice, but by the choice of its creator, the potter.

Thank You, God, for this beautiful collection I have had the privilege of acquiring through the miles and years. Thank You, too, for the reminder that I am formed by You, for Your assigned usefulness. Help me to be content with how You created me and to remain soft and moldable as I am continually being shaped by Your tender hands.

Abandon the Trike

When I was a child, I used to speak like a child, think like a child, reason like a child; when I became a man, I did away with childish things.

1 Corinthians 13:11

As I look out of my kitchen window, an abandoned, and too small anymore, red tricycle sits beside the shop door. Its owner, my grandson, has moved on to bigger, faster wheels; some even battery operated. This was his first training experience. One within his level of safety and adventure, but now mastered. His next level requires greater skills and challenges. Just because he is young doesn't mean he shouldn't try. It is not wrong for a small child to use such a tiny trike. However, as he grows older he should put it away. What a crazy sight it would be if a teenager or a grown man would try to ride this little red three wheeler.

In God's Word we are admonished that yes, when we were children we spoke like a child, understood and thought like a child. Now grown, we must put away and abandon childish things. What a contrast, a transition, from childhood to adulthood. Ultimately, we should grow up, learn and experience life on a more mature level. Kind of like how we start with three wheels, then two, and then move up to four with a motor.

Spiritually, we should always be growing and maturing in the understanding and application of God's Word in our life. Do we desire to remain as an infant spiritually, but all grown up, even gray hair, physically? I pray right now that I will abandon my childish ways, trust God, and allow Him to give me a new set of wheels as I mature in Him.

Thank you, Father, for teaching me daily and giving me new opportunities to grow, for testing me in deeper levels of understanding and application of Your Word. Life in You is so much like learning to ride a bicycle – You start me off slow with training wheels, then as I grow, Your hand gives me a gentle push to venture out to places You will direct me to go; farther and faster with each new lesson.

Ding – Requires a Response

I have called upon You, for You will answer me, O God; incline Your ear to me, hear my speech.
Psalm 17:6

As I look out of my kitchen window, with my hands in warm soapy water, and a mound of dirty dishes to my right, my cell phone dings. I know someone is sending me a text, but my hands are wet so it will just have to wait. Ding again, another reminder for me to read my phone. Read my phone? What happened to verbal communication? Smart phones have become the new norm, even in my old-fashion world. A text or email can be opened to read instantly, hours later or never. All we have to do is just push, slide, or delete. Even my response can be treated the same way by the person on the other end. It is so hard for me to decipher, to truly understand what is being said in these texts; as I cannot see the person's eyes, hear their voice inflection or tone in which they are speaking. I'm still learning all the fun emoji symbols. Lord, have I turned my prayer life, conversations with You, into this way of communicating too? Short sentences I send, read Your reply when I am ready, not busy with hands in dirty dishwater, or in the midst of sinful choices. Push delete when I don't want to hear or answer You. It is sometimes easy to ignore a text till a more convenient time, but an actual voice on the phone requires my acknowledgment, attention, response. I believe that is Your desire for You and me in our communication together – not one sided but interactive, alive, real, and relational. I know that whenever I call to speak to You that You are always there, ready and willing to listen. Ours really is a two-way conversation.

Thank You, for all of this new technology; I really do appreciate the ease and convenience of it. Lord, thank You too, for all the ways, places, and times we communicate together. I am listening and will answer when You call. I am thankful for Your attention when You hear the unending dings of my calls and answer me!

Smoke is the Evidence of Fire

But the Helper, the Holy Spirit, whom the Father will send in My name, He will teach you all things, and bring to your remembrance all that I said to you. Peace I leave with you; My peace I give to you; not as the world gives do I give to you. Do not let your heart be troubled, nor let it be fearful.

John 14:26-27

As I look out of my kitchen window, a light grey ghostlike mist is penetrating low through the pines and around the underbrush, spilling over into the round pen; lightly covering our yard. The flow is so gentle passing through, lingers for a while, and then vanishes within minutes. Smoke, someone must be burning a brush pile in fields close by. It is springtime in our small mountain town and that means burning season. We live in a narrow valley, which is almost like a bowl, as it is almost completely surrounded by mountains. This causes an inversion allowing the smoke or fog to hang a little longer than an area with wind or wide open space. What is stretching before me is the evidence of the fire. It is the result of, not the actual flame. The smoke lets you know by experience that a fire is close by.

I should be that to people around me. I am only alive for a short time, just passing through for a season. My actions will be seen only by those in close proximity to me, soon I will be gone. When people see me, are they experiencing the fire that is burning in me? His name is Jesus. His Holy Spirit lives in me. He is my Helper who teaches me and comforts me. All that I am and all that I do should be seen as the result -- the evidence -- of His power in my life.

I thank You Lord for the presence and power of Your Holy Spirit in my life. I pray that in my season here, my life will draw the attention of others to You.

GUARDING, GUIDING, WATCHING

The Lord is your keeper, the Lord is your shade on your right hand. The sun will not smite you by day, nor the moon by night. The Lord will protect you from all evil; He will keep your soul. The Lord will guard your going out and your coming in from this time forth and forever.

Psalm 121:5-8

As I look out of my kitchen window I laugh out loud; a very young fawn is enjoying a drink from a blue plastic pool just a couple of dozen feet from me. It is not only drinking the water, but standing right in the middle of this child's pool. A few hours ago this same water was filled with my grandsons, splashing, sliding down the miniature slide, squirting each other with orange and green play guns, and fishing for pretend fish with a skinny long stick and yarn. All is quiet and still now, as each has gone home except for this curious deer — now enjoying her own pool time.

As I look past my little friend, in the shadow of the woods stands a larger version of her. It must be the mother, guarding and guiding. She is ready to call at a moment's notice to her young one to run from any danger. My grandchildren were in my care all morning, as I stood on guard, guiding and watching each one as they played. I would call to them from time to time — don't push, slow down before you fall, be careful with the stick so close to your brother's eye. Yes, danger comes in many forms. How wonderful it is for me when I remember my Heavenly Father is always guarding, guiding, and watching me. The fawn, my grandsons, and I must all make the wise choice to obey when we hear the call, which is out of love and concern for our well-being. So much of God's calling is already written down for us, to read, understand, and memorize. Written in the Bible are so many laws and warnings for us to apply to our life in order to escape from danger, or avoid it before it happens. It also has so much encouragement and direction, if heeded we will receive rewards of joy and peace.

We must respond to the one who knows more and sees what we are oblivious to — danger in different forms. The rest of the time we can experience the pleasures of life, knowing He is there as our constant protector.

Thank you, Father, for playtime, laughter, and blue plastic swimming pools. Thank you for the opportunity to not only enjoy my grandchildren but also to protect them. And for reminding me through this fawn, and her mother, how You are always nearby watching me, too.

A Special Room Upstairs

"Do not let your heart be troubled; believe in God, believe also in Me. In My Father's house are many dwelling places; if it were not so, I would have told you; for I go to prepare a place for you. If I go and prepare a place for you, I will come again and receive you to Myself, that where I am, there you may be also. And you know the way where I am going." Thomas said to Him, "Lord, we do not know where You are going, how do we know the way?" Jesus said to him, "I am the way, and the truth, and the life; no one comes to the Father but through Me."

John 14:1-6

As I look out of my kitchen window this rushed morning, I remember the little girl, who years ago rested in the hammock only an arms distance on the other side of this glass. Carefully placed, on the wooden sill is a tri-fold graduation announcement, framing her; now so grown up in these pictures. In one she is wearing a large brimmed hat, with her fingertips touching its sides as it is delicately placed on her head; a faint smile radiates her beauty. In another one she has cameras of different shapes and sizes dangling around her neck. She has deep passion and genuine talent for photography. I am making last minute preparations to be there the moment she walks across the stage; to celebrate with her as she receives her high school diploma. It seems like only days ago my husband and I were preparing, with great excitement, our upstairs room just for her. Not for her to live in our house, but for her own special place. A small room with a tiny dormer window, slanted ceiling, and walls painted yellow. On the largest wall I had enjoyed painting a mural of a field with white flowers, tall green grass, and trees. I remember the smile on her Grandpa's face as he finished building a white picket fence out of wood and attaching it on the adjoining wall; we used it as a headboard for her twin bed. There are still children's books, puzzles, a large wicker basket full of toys, and a doll house with all of the accessories, which was gifted by a coworker of mine just for her. And of course, large, medium, and small teddy bears are all over this child's playroom. Over the years many children have enjoyed this upstairs playroom, but it was prepared for our granddaughter — with love. I will forever cherish the time we have spent together, here in this room, and throughout our cedar house. She lives hours away now, is so grown up, our moments and memories together are less frequent. I pray for her regularly, for her decisions in life, for her love for You, Lord. I pray that the impact I had, and have on her, whether on a road trip, or cooking in the kitchen, or simply being together would always remind her, not only of my great love for her, but of Yours even more. Preparing a room, preparing for trips, preparing many meals, and now for graduation; life is full of preparing for others, but how much of it Lord is focused on You? Is the time we spend preparing for life events with people also filled with moments of preparing our hearts and theirs to trust You? Am I telling, showing, or directing those I love to understand Who You are? How can anyone know the way to the heavenly Father if we do not give them a map? You are the only way, truth, and life; no one gets to enter heaven but through You.

Thank You, Jesus, for going and preparing a place for me in heaven, because of Your great love for me. Thank You that this same promise

is there for anyone who accepts You as Lord and Savior. Not just a cute room with yellow walls, a mural, and a white picket fence, but a mansion and dwelling place with You for all eternity.

Moving Day

For I know the plans that I have for you, declares the Lord, plans for welfare and not for calamity to give you a future and a hope. Then you will call upon Me and come and pray to Me, and I will listen to you. You will seek Me and find Me when you search for Me with all your heart.
Jeremiah 29:11-13

As I look out of my kitchen window with eyes clouded by tears, yet still I try to capture every inch of this view and burn it into my memory forever. My hands instinctively grab the blue and white knitted washcloth out of the hot soapy water as I quickly wipe my countertops for the last time. My thoughts are racing back to the day we moved into this old wood framed house. At that time we had no counters at all, just a piece of plywood with

As I Look Out of My Kitchen Window

a sink dropped in it and some old bookcases that held our dishes, pots, pans, and groceries. How many years we have spent remodeling to get this place just like we wanted – home! Not only a comfortable house, but a home full of memories and love. I think my tears are as much an expression of joy and gratitude for this wonderful place as the sorrow of letting go. I have experienced these same emotions as we have moved from other homes that we had the privilege of living in. Many years ago, on the day we left Alabama to move to Montana, we had left a young man who lived with us as a teenager for about three and a half years. He became an important part of our family. The separation of so many miles, and just life, has kept us apart; but today we are truly blessed to have him here in Montana, by our side, packing and hauling and helping us move again. He and my husband walk into the kitchen after they put the last load on the moving truck. They close it up tight and are ready for our long drive. We walk through our home one last time. These empty rooms were once so full of life. I am very thankful for the memories I hold in my mind and heart as I walk out of each room. We stop for the last time in my kitchen, my back this time is to the window, and we three bow our heads to pray together. We are grateful for all God has given to us, for His great love, for family, and for friends. I look out of my kitchen window one last time and shut the door behind me, as we begin a new chapter in our life, a journey only God knows and has planned out for us. I know His plans are good, as I have experienced them throughout the many years of my life. I also know I must call upon God, listen to Him, and seek Him in order to find Him. He desires my fullest attention and utmost obedience, and then He will answer me. It is then, that His plans can be perfected in my life.

Thank you, Lord, for the many memories that I have had in this beautiful home. Thank You for this special weekend that we spent with family and friends as we packed our last boxes, together. I do not know what the days ahead have in store for me, but I will do my best to seek You first in all that I do. Not my will but Yours, God. I look forward to our new adventures and journeys, together.

It's a Girl!

For You formed my inward parts; You wove me in my mother's womb. I will give thanks to You, for I am fearfully and wonderfully made; wonderful are Your works, and my soul knows it very well. My frame was not hidden from You, when I was made in secret, and skillfully wrought in the depths of the earth; Your eyes have seen my unformed substance; and in Your book were all written the days that were ordained for me, when as yet there was not one of them.

Psalm 139:13-16

As I had looked out of my new kitchen window early this morning, my heart was pounding. I had been moving in such a hurry, my mind full of questions and concerns. I paused for only a moment, looking at the old cross on top of the brown steeple in front of me and quickly prayed, "Lord, please keep her and the baby safe!" Only moments before I was awaken by my husband's tender voice, he showed me a text from our son so many miles away. It simply read: "At the hospital." I knew our grandbaby may come early but this is too early, four weeks too early! I packed as quickly as I could, expecting to drive seven or eight hours and meet our newest grandchild. Traveling for only about an hour and a half, I pulled off the road to read another text from my son: "Her name and weight" and a beautiful picture of her first moments of life. A little farther down the road my excitement soon turned to fear, as the next information I received was they were airlifting her to another hospital. My heart cried out to God, please take care of our precious granddaughter, my daughter-in-law, and son. For many miles today I talked with God about everything and everyone I could think of. The hours of driving seemed to go on forever before I was able to walk into the hospital and meet this oh so tiny member of our family. She is beautiful in every way! Joy and fear are tied up into one big knot in my stomach as I now look at the variety of instruments and tubes; but I also see her strength as her little hand stretches out as if to reach for something, for someone to hold on to. Her long fingers wrap around mine. Only God could create one so small and yet so very full of life.

It's A Girl!

I know that He has been knitting her together inside of her mother from the moment she was conceived. He created her in just the way that pleased Him; He has loved her from her very beginning. Every child who was ever conceived, whether they have breathed their first breath here on earth or not, is precious in His sight and truly loved by Him. My time of prayer and just talking with God began early today at my kitchen window, continued as I looked out of my car window and now praising Him as I stand before this little one I already love so much.

Thank you, Father, for the gift of life, for my own children, their wives, and now the additional blessings of grandchildren! Please, continue to heal my new granddaughter's fragile body, the body You created and now will sustain as You desire. I look forward to many wonderful days of holding, rocking, laughing with, and loving this tiny little girl.

My New Window!

Shout joyfully to the Lord, all the earth. Serve the Lord with gladness; come before Him with joyful singing. Know that the Lord Himself is God; it is He who has made us, and not we ourselves; we are His people and the sheep of His pasture. Enter His gates with thanksgiving and His courts with praise. Give thanks to Him, bless His name. For the Lord is good; His lovingkindness is everlasting and His faithfulness to all generations.

Psalm 100

As I look out of my new kitchen window, a brilliant sunset is reflecting an orange hue onto the brown tiled steeple of the church right next door. The beauty of this moment brings a peace to my chaotic day of unpacking. This is my new window! The view from the small, white framed kitchen window looks out to a tall, narrow steeple pointing toward heaven with a weathered cross on top of it. This is my new place to wash dishes and one more new place to meet with Jesus daily.

Today is almost ending in our new home; a home our church has so graciously provided for us. My mind is wandering to all the many things I need to put away, to clean up, and I realize how easy it is to just stay busy and forget about why I'm here. Not just physically in this state, town, home, but here on earth. I know that God has a purpose for my life. As my eyes glance upward, I am once again keenly aware that my purpose and all that I do should point others to my Father in heaven; just like looking at this steeple draws ones' eyes toward heaven. My life should be a reflection, a beautiful reflection of Him for others.

Thank you, God, for my new window! It will be only one of many places I stop along my busy days to talk with and to listen to You. Thank you, too, for allowing me the privilege of loving and serving You. My life is really not about me, but about serving You!

Author's Note
Your Own Window

Conversations among friends can, and should be, confidential unless otherwise specified. The words you have read on these pages began as very private times, very confidential times between my God and me. Through the years I have written down many of these special talks with God, unaware they would someday be in print.

If you have had an encounter with Jesus that changed your life through the new birth, I pray that you will not only feel and understand my experiences, but that you will look for yourself; for your own quiet places. I pray that your relationship with the Father in heaven will become more personal, intimate, and continually grow. I also pray that you will discover your own window, where you can commune in a new and a fresh way with the Heavenly Father.

If you have never before asked Jesus to be Lord over your life, then there is no better time than now! Not one of us is promised breath tomorrow, so please consider what I'm about to share with you. God's Word, the Bible, says that everyone has sinned and fallen short of God's glory; that the payment for our sin is death for eternity in a place called hell. But God loves you too much to leave you in this condition with no way out. He sent Jesus, His one and only Son, who willingly died a terrible death on an old wooden cross for our sin. Then, just as the Bible says, Jesus rose on the third day and is alive. There is the promise of hope, real life and eternity with Him in heaven for anyone willing to turn away from their sin and turn to Him as Savior! Believing what the Bible says, "Whoever will call on the name of the Lord will be saved" (Romans 10:13) begs you to call upon Him for salvation today!

Bibliography

1. *Gammer Gurton's Garland or the Nursery Parnassus: A Choice Collection of Pretty Songs and Verses,* (London: Harding and Wright, St. John's square, 1810) page 22.

CPSIA information can be obtained
at www.ICGtesting.com
Printed in the USA
FFOW05n1517121117